MW01670713

Published By the Creative House Studio
a division of Black Cotton LLC

Graphic and Layout Editor: Rasta Asaru EL
Photography by: Bruce Conway, Violet Schrage, and Elton Anderson
Book Design by: the Creative House Studio
Edited by: Tiffany King & Janis Powell

ISBN: 978-0-692-09471-6

Printed and bound in the United States

March 2018

First Edition

the CREATIVE HOUSE
Printing & Everything Else

the Creative House Publishing
122 N Market Street
Inglewood, CA 90301
www.thecreativehousestudio.com

Cash In On Cashews

50 Plus Desserts Using One Nut

"Make Love…Eat Dessert"

Chef Babette

Dedication:

I dedicate this book to all of you! If you are reading this book, you more than likely care about the food you consume. Your health is an essential component, but you don't have to sacrifice good taste to be healthy. Bon Appétit

On a personal note, I dedicate this book to my beautiful momma, Inez. I thank her for allowing me to experience her wonderful food and desserts, and for preparing me for where I am today. I know her dream was to own a restaurant. That dream has been manifested through me.

I also dedicate this book to my husband for introducing me to the lifestyle that I live today. It is because of this lifestyle, I am now living my dreams.

Thanks to my management team, The Doyenne Collective as well as Creative House Art Studio who worked tirelessly to help to complete this book.

Last, but not least, to my daughter, LaTrece who translated my "language" (I call it Chef Babette talk!) and helped to take my vision from the kitchen into what you are holding in your hands. Thank you for all the laughs and tears. We finally got it done!

Table of Contents:

Ice Box Desserts

This book is simply about one thing, making incredible,
Ice Box Desserts with one nut… The Cashew…

Let's have some fun and eat what we crave… Sweet Goodness! This book is intended to be a fun, practical and easy guide to building your own delectable Ice Box Desserts. An Ice Box Dessert requires absolutely no baking. It's kind of like making a creamy pudding that morphs into… well just about anything your palate desires. Within minutes you will be creating mouthwatering and visually appealing masterpieces. In this book, you will learn how you can start with a simple base, using one main ingredient, the cashew nut, and turn something simple into absolutely amazing. The sky is the limit with this nut. I choose to work with cashews because I find them to be one of the most versatile and mutable nuts and I am admittedly partial to their delicate and sweet taste. You will discover the many different roles that the cashew nut takes on in this book. I compare it to an A-list actor and definitely the star of the show. After exploring the recipes in this book, you will never view a cashew the same way again… believe me!

I remember when I started playing around with Ice Box Desserts. I started off making parfaits and pies and quickly realized that the cashew was so versatile that I could create almost anything I wanted. The "pies the limit!"—Really! I started off with a simple 6 ingredient recipe, which could stand alone on its own as a parfait, pudding, pie, or ice cream and then I took this basic mix and built upon it. That's the idea of this book; for me to teach you the basics and for you to turn that basic mix into your own "Incredible".

A Little About Chef Babette

It still sounds funny for me to hear others refer to me as a chef. Believe me… That was not my goal growing up. As a matter of fact, I hated cooking. I left all of the cooking to my momma and naively I thought she'd be around forever to cook for me. She was one of the best cooks I knew and I was particularly fond of her desserts. When I was a little girl, she spoiled me with sweets. She would make desserts like sweet potato pie, peach cobbler, and pancakes (affectionately known as "pani-cakes"). She loved to bake cakes. She knew she made people happy with her desserts but she was unaware of the potential health issues associated with her tasty treats. I grew up addicted to sugar and as a result I suffered from common diseases, or as I call it "dis-eases", associated with sugar, like eczema, digestive issues, constipation and symptoms similar to what is known today as Attention Deficit Disorder (ADD).

Many people not only love desserts, but also crave them. After all, sugar is addicting and makes people feel happy no matter what mood they are in. This is why I am so excited about the recipes that are featured in this book. Each dessert makes full use of nutritious, healthy ingredients with many of the beneficial enzymes left intact. I do not use sugar in any of the recipes so there is no worry about the highly addictive downside to sugar consumption or its negative effect on pancreatic function.

In 1990, I met my husband who had a healthy diet at the time. He introduced me to a new way of eating and helped educate me about food and its effects on the body. I started to see and feel a noticeable difference in my health so I began to become more aware of the food I put into it. One of the greatest gifts he gave me was a book entitled, *Fit for Life* by Harvey and Marilyn Diamond. I didn't read the book from beginning to end; instead I would look in the table of contents and find a particular subject that I was interested in and read about it. I did that until I completed the entire book. I woke up one morning and said, "That's it! I'm finished! I'm not eating anymore sugar, dairy or animal flesh and I mean it!" That was about 30 years ago and I look and feel great at age 67.

At the beginning of my transition, I started playing around in the kitchen, trying to imitate tastes that I was familiar with but with healthier ingredients. I was so excited that I started sharing the food with family and friends. I was on a ministry of good health so to speak. I was seeing many of my loved ones suffer from "dis-ease" and I knew if they would only give this lifestyle a chance, they would feel better. Convincing close friends and family was my biggest challenge. They would actually run from me because I was always preaching about the stuff they were eating; but eventually the taste of my food was making a lot of people happy.

I started off as a vendor at City of Angels Church (with the late Reverend O.C. Smith). I then purchased my own food cart and set up shop in front of the Agape Spiritual Center (with Reverend Michael Bernard Beckwith) every Sunday. I spent 6 years there until I finally opened my first restaurant in Inglewood, CA, called *Stuff I Eat*, and I have been sharing great tasting food with the public for 9 years.

I started perfecting the art of vegan desserts after a trip to Sedona, AZ in 2014. I was astonished by the beautiful red rocks and canyons nestled amidst the pine forests. I would wake every morning of my trip to a backdrop of one of the most beautiful natural creations I had ever witnessed. I was also amazed by the beautiful artwork I found in the local businesses, which were inspired by the Sedona topography.

The trip to Sedona was a revelation of sorts, as I realized that I could create art through food. When I returned to my restaurant kitchen, I began recreating some of the memories I had captured on my cell phone. Initially, I would use any fruit or vegetable that I had on hand. My trips to the local farmer's market became more frequent as I realized that the color from the fresh produce enhanced my recipes and helped make the food I serve not only delicious but also beautiful.

I have always expressed my love for art and creativity through music, arts and crafts, and balloon and floral bouquets, but creating beautiful desserts is in my soul. I can spend hours in the kitchen creating masterpieces and now I'm going to share this passion with you!

Meet My Co-Author

Let me introduce you to my co-author, daughter, best friend, and protégé Chef LaTrece Hawkins. She's my hidden gem; and I'm introducing her to all of you because she has worked on this book with me since its inception.

LaTrece studied Health Promotion and Nutrition at University of Southern California. She is passionate about helping women to properly nourish their families. She is currently creating a curriculum and certification course for those looking to incorporate more plant based nutrition into their lives.

The Cashew... This Sweet Nut

Remember I mentioned the star of the show…
The Cashew Nut. I can't say it enough about this truly amazing nut.

History

The cashew nut is native to Brazil. In the 16th Century, Portuguese explorers took cashew trees from Brazil and introduced them to other tropical regions such as India and Africa. Today, the leading commercial producers of cashews are India, Brazil, Mozambique, Tanzania and Nigeria.

Selecting and Storing Cashews

Cashews are available in prepackaged containers or bags. They can also be found in the bulk bin section of your supermarket, but If you choose them from the bulk bin, ensure the bins are covered and that the store has a good product turnover to help ensure freshness. Also search for any evidence of moisture ensure its freshness. and insect damage.

Due to their high content of oleic acid, cashews are more stable than most other nuts but should still be stored in a tightly sealed container in the refrigerator, where they will keep for about six months. They may also be kept in the freezer, where they will keep for about one year.

Health Benefits - Did you know?

Cashews are Heart Protective

Not only do cashews have a lower fat content than most other nuts, approximately 75 percent of their fat is unsaturated fatty acids. Approximately 75 percent of this unsaturated fatty acid content is oleic acid, the same heart-healthy monounsaturated fat found in olive oil.

Cashews Contain Copper

Copper is a great source for antioxidant defenses, energy production, bones and blood vessels.

Cashews are a Great Source of Magnesium

Magnesium is needed for the production of strong bones. A quarter cup of cashews provides 25 percent of the recommended daily value of magnesium.

Cashews Help to Prevent Gallstones

20 years of dietary data collected on 80,000 women from the Nurses' Health Study shows that women who eat at least one ounce of nuts, peanuts or peanut butter each week have a 25 percent lower risk of developing gallstones.

Eating Nuts Lowers the Risk of Weight Gain

A study recently published in September 2017 in the online version of the European Journal of Nutrition has found that people who include nuts in their diet are more likely to reduce weight gain and lower the risk of obesity.

Are Raw Cashews Really Raw?

Actually, the answer is NO. There is a heating process that takes place to remove the nut from the poisonous fruit that houses it; however in the vegan raw community, the “raw” cashew is the one that hasn’t been roasted or salted. This is the one that we will use for our desserts.

Kitchen Essentials

Chef’s Toys

I have found that there are certain equipment and food items that every chef simply can’t live without. The following is a list of items that I have compiled which you may need in order to make the process of preparing these recipes much easier. Don’t feel pressured to go out and buy all of these tools at once. Certain items may be substituted; but in order to get the most out of your prepping experience, the investment is highly recommended.. If you are on a tight budget, by all means use what you have available to you. These brands have become some of my personal favorites, although you may have a particular brand of your own that may be your favorite.

KITCHEN TOOLS FOR DESSERTS FEATURED IN THIS BOOK

Vitamix Blender (High-speed)
Cuisinart Food Processor
Cuisinart Citrus Juicer
Dehydrator (only one recipe)- If you are on a budget and will only use the dehydrator to make the cookies in this book, you can check out the Nesco Snackmaster or the Presto Dehydro. If you plan on being adventurous and doing more, I highly recommend the Excalibur Food Dehydrator.

Measuring Cups

Peelers, Graters and Knives

Wooden Spoons

Mixing Bowls

Scraper

Offset Spatula

Dessert Molds of Choice
(I prefer 3 to 4 inch stainless steel dessert molds, however wherever referenced in this book you can use whatever size molds you prefer)

Zester
Cheese Cloth & Strainers
Below are a list of Ingredients you will need for the recipes in this book. As you scroll through and choose the recipes you would like to try, it might be best to purchase your ingredients in bulk, since you will need them repeatedly.

CONDIMENTS:
Coconut Oil
Cocoa Butter
Raw Cocoa Powder
Sea Salt
Dried Coconut (Sulfur free)
Organic (Alcohol Free) Vanilla Extract
Organic (Alcohol Free) Almond Extract
Organic (Alcohol Free) Lemon Extract

SWEETENERS:
Raw Organic Agave Nectar
Goji Berries
Raisins
Dates

SEEDS:
Chia Seeds
Sunflower Seeds

NUTS: (Organic)
Raw Cashews
Raw Almonds
Raw Walnuts
Raw Pecans

SPICES:
Nutmeg
Cinnamon
Tumeric

Tips, Tricks & Important Information

*****PLEASE READ THIS SECTION BEFORE GETTING STARTED**

If you are anything like me, I'm sure you are probably anxious to flip through this book, find a beautifully pictured dessert and get started but WAIT! I've compiled some important information you should know before moving forward.

• If you have any nut allergies. This is not the book for you. All of the recipes in the book contain nuts; so RUN FAR and FAST or simply give your completed dessert away with LOVE!

Some things you should know about our good friend the Cashew:

• They can be expensive. You can purchase them from the bulk bin and buy cashew pieces, which are less expensive than whole cashews. If you can afford it, always opt for organic.

• When soaking cashews for the recipes, always use distilled or purified water, not from the tap unless it is filtered.

• Cashews should be refrigerated while soaking and should soak for at least 3 hours.

If you are wondering the purpose of "soaking your nuts," (I just had to phrase it that way. Ha!), it's because 1. Nuts contain enzyme inhibitors, which make them difficult to digest. Soaking them usually fixes that. 2. In order to achieve the consistency you need for the desserts in this book, you need a soft nut. Who likes hard nuts? I just had to say that too. Ha again!

You can store soaked cashews in the refrigerator for future use. They will become very slimy and will smell fermented but are still good to use. Simply rinse them before use. Soaked cashews will keep in the refrigerator at a consistent chilled temperature for up to 2 weeks.

Most of the recipes in this book call for a parfait. Many times you will have extra mix leftover. There are quite a few things you can do with your parfait mix:

• Turn it into a simple yogurt by transferring the parfait mix to a clean glass jar (like a mason jar) Add a serving of probiotic acidophilus, then cover with plastic wrap, secured by a rubber band. Allow the parfait mix to sit in a warm place for at least 24 hours or until it ferments, and Voila! Of course you will want to refrigerate it after you have achieved this. Another cool thing you can do is to freeze your leftovers and make ice cream. Yum!!!

I love to add nutritional yeast to the pie recipes. If you are not familiar with nutritional yeast, for us vegans it helps things to taste cheesy, so if you are looking to make cheesecake, simply add a tablespoon or two (to taste) and turn a pie into a cheesecake.

DO NOT DISCARD YOUR RIPE AVOCADO. I used to despise dark spotted avocado, but now I love them. They make the best chocolate pudding and you will use them for many of the recipes in this book. So treasure these little guys.

A note about Baby Thai coconut. First… Be careful opening it. There are many YouTube tutorials that demonstrate this. If you don't think you can open one without inuring yourself you can ask someone braver than you or simply use a can of organic coconut milk plus the cream on top. Visit *happyhappyvegan.com* for tips on how to select this delicious nut. Coconut offers these recipes a distinctive taste. Feel free to replace coconut for any recipe that only calls for non-dairy milk. I used to use them in all my recipes but for simplicity sake. Non-dairy milk has become one of my best friends. The choice is yours. Remember this is just a guide.

Speaking of organic, assume that all the recipes are organic. I believe in it. Visit your local farmers market and become familiar with the farmers and their product. Play with produce you have never experienced before and create your own masterpieces!

If you want any of the parfait mixes to be thicker, simply use 1/4 cup less non-dairy milk.

You are more than welcomed to mix flavors. The following are some of my favorite flavor combinations but feel free to create your own:

- -Strawberry/Lemon
- -Lemon/Pineapple
- -Blueberry/Lemon
- -Chocolate/Peanut Butter

Anytime you are working with crust and it doesn't mold to your pan or dish, simply add more parfait mix or agave nectar to achieve a consistency you can work with.

You don't have to make granola for these recipes. You can purchase any granola you like as long as the ingredients are clean (no junk or weird ingredients). My favorite store bought granola is,

Natures Path Organic Hemp Granola.

A few of the recipes call for melted cocoa butter. I don't use microwaves, so a trick that I have found (if you don't own a double broiler) is to boil a 1/2 cup of water in a small pot and place the hard cubed cocoa butter in a metal measuring cup and place the entire cup in the center of the pot until it melts. It's quick and simple.

Here is a trick for creating a rich red color from beet juice. Simply peel a fresh beet, cut it into quarters and put it in the blender with the amount of water needed for the recipe and blend. Strain the pulp and there you have it. Let's call it "cheat juice". The richness of beets is a great flavor and color enhancer.

Chapter 1

Ice Box Parfaits

Ice Box Parfaits

The Base Parfait

The base parfait recipe serves as the catalyst for all the other recipes listed within this book. Once you've mastered the base, it will become as simple as adding your desired flavor and the base transforms the taste to as little or as dramatic as your taste buds desire. It's as simple as 1-2-3. But in this case, 1-2-3-4-5-6!

Equipment:

High-speed blender
Spatula
Cup or bowl
Measuring cup
Measuring spoons

Products:

Non-dairy milk
Raw cashews
Agave nectar
Coconut oil
Sea salt
Vanilla extract

Ingredients:

1 cup non-dairy milk
2 cups raw soaked cashews (rinsed)
3/4 cup agave nectar (sweetened to taste)
1/2 tsp. sea salt
1 tsp. vanilla extract
1/4 cup coconut oil

Instructions: Add all liquids to the blender first and then all other ingredients. Combine in a high speed blender and blend until smooth and creamy. Allow the parfait to chill in the refrigerator for 20-30 minutes until firm. Garnish with desired fruit, nuts or granola.

*Note: Add 2 tbsp. of lemon juice and any fruit to the base parfait recipe to transform it into a new flavor. ***For a thicker base add less milk (3/4 cup).*

Okay! Let's have some fun!!! We are simply going to take the base parfait and transform it into different desserts.

LEMON PARFAIT

Equipment:

- High-speed blender
- Spatula
- Cup or bowl
- Measuring cup
- Measuring spoons

Products:

- Non-dairy milk
- Raw cashews
- Lemon (1-2 lemons depending on size and density)
- Agave nectar
- Coconut oil
- Sea salt
- Vanilla extract

Ingredients:

- 1/2 cup lemon juice
- 1/2 cup non-dairy milk
- 2 cups cashews
- 3/4 cup agave nectar
- ½ tsp. sea salt
- 1 tsp. lemon extract (non-alcohol)
- ¼ cup coconut oil

Instructions: Add all liquids to the blender first and then add all other ingredients. Combine in a high-speed blender until smooth and creamy. Allow the parfait to chill in the refrigerator for 20-30 minutes until firm. Garnish with desired fruit, nuts or granola.

Note***For a thicker base add less milk (3/4 cup).

STRAWBERRY PARFAIT

Equipment:

High-speed blender
Spatula
Cup or bowl
Measuring cup
Measuring spoons

Products:

Non-dairy milk
Raw cashews (2 lbs may not need all, freeze leftovers for future desserts)
Lemons
Frozen Strawberries (1 large bag)
Beets (juice 2 medium beets or cut them up,
blend with water and put through a strainer)
Agave nectar
Coconut oil
Sea salt
Vanilla extract

Ingredients:

*Add the following ingredients to the lemon parfait mix
(pg. 25 minus lemon extract)
2 cups fresh or frozen strawberries
2 tbsp. beet juice
(optional for a richer color- see Tips, Tricks and Important Information).

Instructions: Add all liquids to the blender first and then add all other ingredients. Combine in a high-speed blender until smooth and creamy. Allow the parfait to chill in the refrigerator for 20-30 minutes until firm. Garnish with desired fruit, nuts or granola.

*Note: ***For a thicker base add less milk (3/4 cup)*

KEY LIME PARFAIT

Equipment:

High-speed blender
Spatula
Cup or bowl
Measuring cup
Measuring spoons

Products:

Non-dairy milk
Raw cashews
Limes (4)
Kiwi (2)
Agave nectar
Coconut oil
Sea salt
Vanilla extract

Ingredients:

1/2 cup non-dairy milk
1/2 cup lime juice
2 peeled kiwi
2 tbsp. lime zest (4 limes)
2 cups soaked and rinsed cashews
1 cup agave nectar
2 tbsp. coconut oil
½ tsp. sea salt
1 tsp. vanilla extract

Instructions: Add all liquids to the blender first and then add all other ingredients. Combine in a high-speed blender until smooth and creamy. Allow the parfait to chill in the refrigerator for 20-30 minutes until firm. Garnish with desired fruit, nuts or granola.

Note: ***For a thicker base add less milk (3/4 cup)

RASPBERRY PARFAIT

Equipment:

High-speed blender
Spatula
Cup or bowl
Measuring cup
Measuring spoons

Products:

Non-dairy milk
Raw cashews
Lemons (4 lemons - may not use them all depending on preferred tartness)
Frozen raspberries (1-2 bags depending on size)
Freeze dried raspberries (1 bag)
Agave nectar
Coconut oil
Sea salt
Vanilla extract

Ingredients:

*Add the following ingredients to the lemon parfait mix
(pg. 25 minus lemon extract)
* For a less tart taste add less lemon juice (1/4 cup)
2 cups fresh or frozen raspberries
1 bag freeze dried raspberries for a richer color and taste.

Instructions: Add all liquids to the blender first and then add all other ingredients. Combine in a high-speed blender until smooth and creamy. Allow the parfait to chill in the refrigerator for 20-30 minutes until firm. Garnish with desired fruit, nuts or granola.

*Note: ***For a thicker base add less milk (3/4 cup)*

BLUEBERRY PARFAIT

Equipment:

High-speed blender
Spatula
Cup or bowl
Measuring cup
Measuring spoons

Products:

Non-dairy milk
Raw cashews
Lemons (2)
Fresh or frozen blueberries (1 bag)
Freeze dried blueberries (1 bag)
Agave nectar
Coconut oil
Sea salt
Vanilla extract

Ingredients:

*Add the following ingredients to the lemon parfait mix (pg. 25 minus lemon extract)
* For a less tart taste add less lemon juice (1/4 cup)
2 cups fresh or frozen blueberries
1 bag freeze dried blueberries for a richer color and taste

Instructions: Add all liquids to the blender first and then add all other ingredients. Combine in a high-speed blender until smooth and creamy. Allow the parfait to chill in the refrigerator for 20-30 minutes until firm. Garnish with desired fruit, nuts or granola.

Note: ***For a thicker base add less milk (3/4 cup)

BANANA PARFAIT

Equipment:

High-speed blender
Spatula
Cup or bowl
Measuring cup
Measuring spoons

Products:

Non-dairy milk
Raw cashews
Lemons (1)
Bananas (3 ripe)
Agave nectar
Coconut oil
Sea salt
Vanilla extract

Ingredients:

*Add the following ingredients to the base parfait mix (pg. 23)
3 ripe bananas (preference is spotted for a sweeter taste and less starch)
2 tbsp. lemon juice

Instructions: Add all liquids to the blender first and then add all other ingredients. Combine in a high-speed blender until smooth and creamy. Allow the parfait to chill in the refrigerator for 20-30 minutes until firm. Garnish with desired fruit, nuts or granola.

Note: ***For a thicker base add less milk (3/4 cup)

APPLE PARFAIT

Equipment:

High-speed blender
Spatula
Cup or bowl
Measuring cup
Measuring spoons

Products:

Non-dairy milk
Raw cashews
Lemons (1)
Unsulfured dried apples (1 bag)
Agave nectar
Coconut oil
Sea salt
Vanilla extract

Ingredients:

*Add the following ingredients to the base parfait mix (pg. 23)
2 tbsp. lemon juice
2 cups (unsulfured) dried apples that have been soaked for at least 30 minutes in warm water.

Instructions: Add all liquids to the blender first and then add all other ingredients. Combine in a high-speed blender until smooth and creamy. Allow the parfait to chill in the refrigerator for 20-30 minutes until firm. Garnish with desired fruit, nuts or granola.

Note: ***For a thicker base add less milk (3/4 cup)

MILK CHOCOLATE PARFAIT

Equipment:

High-speed blender
Spatula
Cup or bowl
Measuring cup
Measuring spoons

Products:

Non-dairy milk
Raw cashews
Agave nectar
Coconut oil
Cocoa powder
Sea salt
Vanilla extract

Ingredients:

*Add the following ingredients to the base parfait mix (pg. 23)
¼ cup cocoa powder
(for a richer chocolate taste, add more cocoa powder 1/2 cup)

Instructions: Add all liquids to the blender first and then add all other ingredients. Combine in a high-speed blender until smooth and creamy. Allow the parfait to chill in the refrigerator for 20-30 minutes until firm. Garnish with desired fruit, nuts or granola.

Note: ***For a thicker base add less milk (3/4 cup)

WHITE CHOCOLATE PARFAIT

Equipment:

High-speed blender
Spatula
Cup or bowl
Measuring cup
Measuring spoons

Products:

Non-dairy milk
Raw cashews
Agave nectar
Coconut oil
Cocoa butter
Sea salt
Vanilla extract

Ingredients:

*Add the following ingredients to the base parfait mix (pg. 23)
1/2 cup melted cocoa butter or (5-6 cubes)

***Note - cocoa butter must be melted in a double broiler for proper measurement.

If you do not own a double broiler you can use my trick… Add cocoa butter to a metal measuring cup and place in a shallow pot of boiling water until butter is melted.

Instructions: Add all liquids to the blender first and then add all other ingredients. Combine in a high-speed blender until smooth and creamy. Allow the parfait to chill in the refrigerator for 20-30 minutes until firm. Garnish with desired fruit, nuts or granola.

Note: ***For a thicker base add less milk (3/4 cup)

MANGO PARFAIT

Equipment:

High-speed blender
Spatula
Cup or bowl
Measuring cup
Measuring spoons

Products:

Non-dairy milk
Raw cashews
Lemons (1-2 depending on preferred tartness)
Fresh or frozen mango
Agave nectar
Coconut oil
Sea salt
Vanilla extract
Turmeric

Ingredients:

*Add the following ingredients to the lemon parfait mix (pg. 25 minus lemon extract)
2 cups fresh or frozen mango
1/2 tsp. turmeric (optional for a richer color)
For a less tart taste add less lemon juice (1/4 cup)

Instructions: Add all liquids to the blender first and then add all other ingredients. Combine in a high-speed blender until smooth and creamy. Allow the parfait to chill in the refrigerator for 20-30 minutes until firm. Garnish with desired fruit, nuts or granola.

Note: ***For a thicker base add less milk (3/4 cup)

PEACH PARFAIT

Equipment:

High-speed blender
Spatula
Cup or bowl
Measuring cup
Measuring spoons

Products:

Non-dairy milk
Raw cashews
Lemons (1-2 depending on preferred tartness)
Fresh or frozen peaches (1-2 bags depending on size)
Agave nectar
Coconut oil
Sea salt
Vanilla extract

Ingredients:

*Add ingredients to the lemon parfait mix (pg. 25 minus lemon extract)
* For a less tart taste add less lemon juice (1/4 cup)
2 cups fresh or frozen peach

Instructions: Add all liquids to the blender first and then add all other ingredients. Combine in a high- speed blender until smooth and creamy. Allow the parfait to chill in the refrigerator for 20-30 minutes until firm. Garnish with desired fruit, nuts or granola.

Note:***For a thicker base add less milk (3/4 cup)

PEANUT BUTTER PARFAIT

Equipment:

High-speed blender
Spatula
Cup or bowl
Measuring cup
Measuring spoons

Products:

Non-dairy milk
Raw cashews (1lb bag)
Agave nectar
Coconut oil
Roasted, non-salted peanut butter
Sea salt
Vanilla extract

Ingredients:

*Add ingredients to the base parfait mix (pg. 23)
3/4 cup organic, roasted, non-salted peanut butter

****Note: Organic peanut butter contains a lot of oil that usually settles at the top of the container. Be sure to stir your peanut butter thoroughly to incorporate the oil into the peanut butter prior to use.*

Instructions: Add all liquids to the blender first and then add all other ingredients. Combine in a high-speed blender until smooth and creamy. Allow the parfait to chill in the refrigerator for 20-30 minutes until firm. Garnish with desired fruit, nuts or granola.

Note: ***For a thicker base add less milk (3/4 cup)

nature's all
ORGANIC
RASPBERRIES

HOLIDAY PARFAITS

*S*erve your guests a little something special with these holiday treats. Feel free to transform any of these parfaits into a pie or cake by simply creating a crust. Look in the pie or cake chapters for ideas and get creative.

CRANBERRY PARFAIT

Equipment:

High-speed blender
Spatula
Cup or bowl
Measuring cup
Measuring spoons

Products:

Non-dairy milk
Raw cashews
Lemons (1-2 depending on preferred tartness)
Fresh cranberries (1-2 bags depending on size)
Agave nectar
Coconut oil
Sea salt
Vanilla extract

Ingredients:

*Add ingredients to the lemon parfait mix (pg. 25 minus lemon extract)
2 cups fresh cranberries
* For a less tart taste add less lemon juice (1/4 cup)

Instructions: Add all liquids to the blender first and then add all other ingredients. Combine in a high-speed blender until smooth and creamy. Allow the parfait to chill in the refrigerator for 20-30 minutes until firm. Garnish with desired fruit, nuts or granola.

Note: ***For a thicker base add less milk (3/4 cup)

SWEET POTATO PARFAIT

Equipment:

High-speed blender
Spatula
Cup or bowl
Measuring cup
Measuring spoons

Products:

Non-dairy milk
Raw cashews
Lemons (1)
Yam (1 medium)
Agave nectar
Coconut oil
Sea salt
Vanilla extract
Nutmeg

Ingredients:

*Add ingredients to the base parfait mix (pg. 23 minus lemon extract)
1 tbsp. lemon juice
1 tsp. nutmeg
1 medium yam (peeled and cubed)

Instructions: Add all liquids to the blender first and then add all other ingredients. Combine in a high-speed blender until smooth and creamy. Allow the parfait to chill in the refrigerator for 20-30 minutes until firm. Garnish with desired fruit, nuts or granola.

Note: ***For a thicker base add less milk (3/4 cup)

NOT SO EGGNOG PARFAIT

Equipment:

High-speed blender
Spatula
Cup or bowl
Measuring cup
Measuring spoons

Products:

Non-dairy milk
Raw cashews
Agave nectar
Dates (1 bag pitted)
Coconut oil
Sea salt
Cinnamon
Ground cloves
Vanilla extract

Ingredients:

*Add ingredients to the base parfait mix (pg. 25 minus lemon extract)
6 Medjool (pitted) dates
1/4 Cup Agave
1 tsp. nutmeg
1 pinch cinnamon
1 pinch ground cloves

Instructions: Add all liquids to the blender first and then add all other ingredients. Combine in a high-speed blender until smooth and creamy. Allow the parfait to chill in the refrigerator for 20-30 minutes until firm. Garnish with desired fruit, nuts or granola.

.

Note: ***For a thicker base add less milk (3/4 cup)

IF you're Wishing and Hoping and Thinking and Praying you could still eat desserts, well now you can… Bon Appėtit!

--Chef Babette

Chapter 2

Ice Box Puddings

CITRUS PUDDING

Equipment:

- High-speed blender
- Spatula
- Cup or bowl
- Measuring cup
- Measuring spoons

Products:

- Non-dairy milk
- Raw cashews
- Lime (2-3 depending on size)
- Avocado (3)
- Agave nectar
- Coconut oil
- Sea salt
- Vanilla extract

Ingredients:

- 3 ripe avocados (***Avocado should be soft with no dark spots)
- 1 cup lemon parfait mix (pg. 25))
- ¼ cup lime juice
- ½ cup agave syrup (sweeten to taste)
- 1 tsp. vanilla extract
- 2 tbsp. coconut oil
- 1 tsp. sea salt

Instructions: Add all liquids to the blender first and then add all other ingredients. Combine in a high- speed blender until smooth and creamy. Allow the pudding to chill in the refrigerator for 20-30 minutes until firm. Garnish with desired fruit, nuts or granola.

Note: ***This is a stand-alone pudding and can be eaten without the parfait mix added to it. The cashews in the parfait mix give it a key lime pie vibe.

DARK CHOCOLATE PUDDING

Have you ever wondered what to do with your spotted avocado? This recipe is the answer. Never throw another one away.

Equipment:

High-speed blender
Spatula
Cup or bowl
Measuring cup
Measuring spoons

Products:

Non-dairy milk
Raw cashews
Lemons
Avocado (4 ripe)
Cocoa powder (1 bag/box)
Agave nectar
Coconut oil
Sea salt
Vanilla extract

Ingredients:

4 ripe avocados (ripe and spotted avocado are fine to use)
¼ cup cocoa powder (more cocoa powder for a richer and darker pudding or less for a milder taste).
½ cup agave nectar
2 tbsp. coconut oil
1/2 tsp. sea salt
1 tsp. vanilla extract
1/2 Cup Soaked Cashews (rinsed)

Instructions: Add all liquids to the blender first and then add all other ingredients. Combine in a high-speed blender until smooth and creamy. Allow the pudding to chill in the refrigerator for 20-30 minutes until firm. Garnish with Sweet Cashew Crumble. (See pg. 139).

Get serious! Get started! Get moving! Get ready… For the change.

--Chef Babette

BANANA PUDDING

Equipment:

High-speed blender
Spatula
Cup or bowl
Measuring cup
Measuring spoons

Products:

Non-dairy milk
Raw cashews (1-2 lb bag)
Lemons (1)
Agave nectar
Coconut oil
Sea salt
Vanilla extract
Bananas (3)
Hemp Granola (I box) or Vegan Vanilla Wafers

Ingredients:

2 cups raw soaked cashews (rinsed)
3 ripe bananas
1 cup non dairy milk
½ tsp. lemon juice
1/4 cup coconut oil
1/2 tsp. sea salt
1 tsp. vanilla extract
½ cup agave nectar

Instructions: Add all liquids to the blender first and then add all other ingredients. Combine in a high-speed blender until smooth and creamy. Allow the pudding to chill in the refrigerator for 20-30 minutes until firm.

Assembly:

(For a single serving)
1. Layer bowl with choice of granola (Hemp is my favorite) or a vegan vanilla wafer of your choice.
2. Add 3 tbsp. of pudding
3. Slice banana to cover layer of pudding
4. Add 4 tbsp. of pudding (top layer)

Note: ***Feel free to layer this pudding however you desire your banana pudding. Less or more pudding is a matter of preference.

CARAMEL PUDDING

Equipment:

High-speed blender
Spatula
Cup or bowl
Measuring cup
Measuring spoons

Products:

Non-dairy milk
Raw cashews (1-2 lb bag)
Lemons
Agave nectar
Dates (1 lb of pitted dates)
Coconut oil
Sea salt
Vanilla Extract

Ingredients:

1 cup non-dairy milk
2 cups raw soaked cashews (rinsed)
3/4 cup caramel sauce (please see caramel sauce recipe pg. 142)
1/2 tsp. sea salt
1 tsp. vanilla extract
1/4 cup coconut oil
2 cups of pitted dates
1/2 cup agave nectar

Instructions: Add all liquids to the blender first and then add all other ingredients. Combine in a high-speed blender and blend until smooth and creamy. Allow the parfait to chill in the refrigerator for 20-30 minutes until firm. Then place in desired serving glasses/dish. Garnish with desired fruit, nuts or granola.

CHIA SEED PUDDING

Equipment:

High-speed blender
Spatula
Cup or bowl
Measuring cup
Measuring spoons

Products:

Non-dairy milk
Raw cashews (1-2 bags depending on size)
Agave nectar
Coconut oil
Sea salt
Cinnamon
Chia Seeds (1 bag)
Vanilla extract

Ingredients:

1 cup non-dairy milk
2 cups raw soaked cashews (rinsed)
3/4 cup agave nectar (sweetened to taste)
1/2 tsp. sea salt
1 tsp. vanilla extract
1 tsp. cinnamon
2 tbsp. chia seeds
1/4 cup coconut oil

Instructions: Add all liquids to the blender and then add all other ingredients EXCEPT CHIA SEEDS. Combine in a high-speed blender and blend until smooth and creamy. Transfer to a mixing bowl and incorporate chia seeds into the pudding. Allow pudding to chill in the refrigerator for 20-30 minutes until firm.

CHAPTER 3
Ice Box Pies

KIWI KEY LIME PIE

I could never decide just how to make pies with kiwi, but after realizing that I already had lime flavored pie mix, I thought I'd add a few kiwi's to the mix for a tasty Kiwi Key Lime pie! What a great decision that was; this pie is fabulous! My momma used to say, "it's a poor frog that won't praise his own pond". Well I must praise myself because I am simply beside myself every time I bite into this mouthwatering treat.

Equipment:

- 8" pie dish
- Citrus juicer
- Zester
- Measuring cups and spoons
- High-speed blender
- Food processor
- Bowls
- Knife
- Spatula

Products:

- Limes (6 limes)
- Kiwi (2)
- Raw cashews (1lb)
- Raw almonds (1lb)
- Agave nectar
- Non-dairy milk
- Sea salt
- Coconut oil
- Vanilla extract

Kiwi Key Lime Filling:

- 1 cup non-dairy milk
- 2 peeled kiwi
- 1 cup lime juice
- 1-2 ripe avocado (not spotted)
- 2 tbsp. lime zest (4 limes)
- 2 1/2 cups soaked cashews
- 1 1/2 cup agave nectar
- 2 tbsp. coconut oil
- 1/2 tsp. sea salt
- 1 tsp. vanilla extract

Crust:

- 2 cups raw almonds
- 1 tbsp. cup coconut oil
- 2 tbsp. agave nectar
- 1 tsp. vanilla extract
- 1/2 tsp. sea salt

Instructions: Add all liquids to the blender first and add then all other ingredients. Combine in a high-speed blender and blend until smooth and creamy. Allow the filling to chill in the refrigerator for 20-30 minutes until firm.

Place all almonds in food processor using the S-Blade and break the nuts down to a grainy consistency. Transfer the crust to a bowl and add the remaining ingredients. The crust should become slightly sticky so that it forms well to pie pan.

Assembly:
Spray the pie dish lightly with non-stick oil spray and form the crust in pie dish, add filling and freeze until firm. Decorate with kiwi and lime slices prior to serving.

Eat Life to sustain life
--**Chef Babette**

“CHA CHA” KEY LIME MINI PIES

Looking for something sexy? This is it! With a few tweaks, we are transforming the key lime pie into a sensual, romantic and flirty dessert. Think of a beautiful Latin ballroom dancer performing the “Cha Cha.” Yes, this is indeed the quintessential sexy dessert. I know I feel sexy eating this dessert, especially because I never have to worry about losing my girlish figure since this muchacha is only going to enhance what I'm already working with. So put your heels on and “Cha Cha Cha!”

Equipment:

- Citrus juicer
- Citrus zester
- High-speed blender
- Round mold ring (1-1/2 inches)
- Food processor
- Measuring cups
- Measuring spoons
- Non-stick cookie sheet

Products:

- Limes
- Raw cashews, soaked and dry, (1 bag)
- Agave nectar
- Vanilla extract
- Coconut oil
- Baby Thai coconut
- Sea salt

Crust:

- 1 cup raw cashews
- 2 tbsp. coconut oil
- 2 tbsp. agave nectar
- 1/2 tsp. sea salt

Place the dry cashews in food processor using the S-Blade and break the nuts down to a grainy consistency. Transfer the cashews to a bowl and add the remaining ingredients. The crust should become slightly sticky. Spray each mold with non-stick oil. Remove the mixture from the processor. Flatten the crust to a 1/4 inch thickness inside the bottom of each mold. Place the molds in the freezer until the crust is firm. During this time, proceed to prepare the filling.

Filling:

Baby Thai Coconut (use entire coconut water and spoon out meat)

1 cup lime juice
2 lime zest (4 limes)
4 cups soaked cashews
1-1/2 cup Agave nectar
2 tbsp. coconut oil
1/2 tsp. sea salt
1 tsp. vanilla powder

Instructions: Add all liquids and coconut flesh to the blender first and then add all other ingredients. Combine in a high-speed blender and blend until smooth and creamy. Allow the filling to chill in the refrigerator for 20-30 minutes until firm.

Assembly:

Remove crust from freezer and pour filling into 1 1/2 inch round mold ring onto crust and place in the freezer until firm (approx. 2-3 hrs.). To remove from mold, place a warm cloth around the mold until dessert slides out. Garnish with fresh fruit, mint, and serve.

Just a spoonful of cashews can go a long way. But remember soak nuts first.

--Chef Babette

RAW SWEET POTATO / PECAN CARAMEL PIE

Now ya'll know I had to include a raw sweet potato pie. I absolutely loved sweet potato pie while I was growing up and my mom's was especially delectable. Her crust was as light as a feather and her filling was a warm, sweet custard that melted in your mouth. Once I became vegan I had no clue how I was going to replace that taste but I must say I'm pretty satisfied with my creation. I love to dress my version up with caramel sauce and pecans. It gives them that sweet potato, pecan vibe.

Equipment:

High-speed blender
Food processor S-Blade
Measuring cups and spoons
Bowls
Spatula
Pie pan
Potato peeler

Products:

Cashews
Yams (1 medium)
Either carrot juice/ almond milk/ coconut milk
Lemons (1)
Agave nectar
Sea salt
Nutmeg
Vanilla powder
Pecans (1 lb)
Coconut oil

Crust:

2 cups ground pecans
1/2 tsp. sea salt

1 tbsp. coconut oil
2 tbsp. agave nectar

Place pecans in food processor using the S-Blade and break the nuts down to a grainy consistency. Transfer the crust to a bowl and add remaining ingredients. The crust should become slightly sticky so that it forms well to pie pan.

Raw Sweet Potato Pie Filling:

1 medium yam (diced)
1 1/2 cups soaked and rinsed cashews
1 1/2 cup carrot juice or almond milk
1/4 cup coconut oil
3/4 cup agave nectar (to taste)
2 tbsp. lemon juice
1 tsp. sea salt
1 tsp. nutmeg
1/2 tsp. vanilla extract

Instructions:

Add all liquids to the blender first and then add all other ingredients. Combine in a high-speed blender and blend until smooth and creamy.

Assembly:

Spray pie pan with non-stick oil spray. Firmly shape the crust to the pie pan and add filling. Place in the freezer for 3-5 hours or until firm. This dessert can be eaten as is or with the caramel topping. (See caramel recipe pg. 142).

It's never to late to begin your journey to a better and healthier you.

--**Chef Babette**

PEANUT BUTTER YAM PIE

Equipment:

High-speed blender
Food processor S-Blade
Measuring cups and spoons
Bowls
Spatula
Pie Pan
Potato Peeler

Products:

Cashews (1-2 bags depending on size)
Yams (1-2 depending on size)
Either carrot Juice/ almond milk/ coconut milk
Agave nectar
Sea salt
Nutmeg
Vanilla extract
Creamy peanut butter (1 jar)
Hemp granola (2 lb bag)
Coconut oil
Non-stick oil spray

Crust:

3 cups hemp granola
2 tbsp. peanut butter yam filling (see recipe below)

Mix well until Granola is coated. Place the granola on the bottom and the sides of a 1/4 inch thick pie dish and set aside.

Peanut Butter Yam Filling:

1 cup non dairy milk (carrot or almond, your preference)
1/2 cup creamy peanut butter
1 cup soft yams (boil) to begin to soften

3/4 cup agave nectar
1 tsp. nutmeg
1 tsp. sea salt
2 tsp. vanilla extract
2 1/2 cups soaked and rinsed cashews
1/4 cup coconut oil

Instructions:
Add all liquids to the blender first and then add all other ingredients. Combine in a high-speed blender and blend until smooth and creamy.

Assembly:
Spray the pie pan with non-stick oil spray. Firmly shape the crust to the pie pan, add the filling on top of the crust. Put the pie pan in the freezer and allow to become firm (3-5 hours). Take it out of the freezer and drizzle with caramel sauce (See pg. 142).

CHOCOLATE SWEET POTATO PIE

Now it's time to get "jazzy" with our raw sweet potato. Are you ready for this? Yes... We are adding chocolate. Can you say yum!!!

Using the sweet potato pie recipe and the dark chocolate pudding, we are going to make a completely different dessert.

Crust:

- 2 cups ground pecans
- ½ tsp. sea salt
- 2 tbsp. cocoa powder
- 1 tbsp. coconut oil
- 2 tbsp. agave nectar

Place pecans in food processor using the S-Blade and break the nuts down to a grainy consistency. Transfer crust to a bowl and add remaining ingredients. The crust should become slightly sticky so that it forms well to the pie pan.

Assembly:
Spray the pie pan with non-stick oil spray. Firmly shape the crust to pie pan. Add the chocolate pudding mix as the 2nd layer. Put in the freezer and allow to become firm (30 min). Take out of the freezer and add sweet potato pie mix as 3rd layer. Put the pie back in the freezer and allow to become completely firm (2-3 hours). After the pie is completely firm, decorate the top with chocolate pudding by adding the pudding to a plastic baggie (cut a small hole in the corner and squeeze) or use a decorating tube if available. Garnish with carob chips if desired. Be creative and have fun!!!

MANGO LEMON PIE

Equipment:

High-speed blender
Food processor S-Blade
Measuring cups and spoons
Bowls
Spatula
9” Pie Dish (your preference)

***Product*:**

Cashews
Lemons (1 large)
Organic coconut milk in the can (or any non-dairy milk)
2 fresh mango (or 1 8oz bag frozen)
Agave nectar
Sea salt
Coconut oil
Granola (bag)
Non-stick oil spray
Organic dried mango (1 bag)
Walnuts (1 bag)

***Crust*:**

1 cup granola
1 cup walnuts
1 tbsp. coconut oil
2 tbsp. agave
2 tbsp. lemon juice
1/2 tsp. sea salt

Process (on pulse) the granola, walnuts and sea salt until grainy. Add agave, coconut oil and lemon juice, leaving the mixture slightly grainy. Add crust to the bottom and sides of a 9” pie dish.

Lemon Pie Filling: (See lemon parfait recipe, pg. 25).

Mango Pie Filling:

1 cup non dairy milk
3/4 cups agave
2 tbsp. lemon
1 cup organic dried mango (soaked until soft)
1 cup frozen or 2 fresh mango
1/4 cup coconut oil
1 tsp. sea salt
2 1/2 cups soaked and rinsed cashews

Instructions:

Add all liquids to the blender first and then add all other ingredients. Combine in a high-speed blender and blend until smooth and creamy.

Assembly:

Spray the pie pan with non-stick oil spray. Firmly shape the crust to the pie pan. Add lemon parfait filling and put the pie in the freezer and allow it to become firm (2 hours). Take the pie out of freezer and add the mango mix and diced mango. Place it back in the freezer until firm. Garnish with fresh mango if desired.

STRAWBERRY PIE

I can't help but crave this creamy deliciousness paired with fresh, juicy strawberries. Can you say, "yummy goodness?" This pie is similar to cheesecake. As a matter of fact, if you desire a cream cheese taste you will simply add the secret ingredient, nutritional yeast. Yes It's as easy as that! Now, everyone knows that cheesecake lovers are genuinely pretty picky and they all have their favorite type: New York style, Chicago style, Philadelphia style, and baked versus unbaked; and of course raw. The versatility of this creamy pie is amazing and once again our good friend the cashew takes us to the places we want to go. Enjoy!

Equipment:

High-speed blender
Food processor S-Blade
Measuring cups and spoons
Bowls
Spatula
Pie Pan

Product:

Cashews (1-2 bags depending on size)
Pecans (1-2 bags depending on size)
Lemons
Baby Thai coconut (1)
Lemons (3-4 lemons)
Fresh strawberries (1-2 lbs) Frozen strawberries (1-2 bags depending on size)
Agave nectar
Nutritional yeast (optional)
Sea alt
Coconut oil
Granola
Non-stick oil spray

 Crust:

2 cups ground pecans
1/2 tsp. sea salt
1 tbsp. coconut oil
2 tbsp. agave nectar

Place all ingredients in the food processor using the S-Blade and break the nuts down to a grainy consistency.

Strawberry Pie Filling:

1 coconut (water and coconut meat)
1 cup lemon juice
2 tbsp. coconut oil
3 cups soaked cashews
1 1/2 cup agave nectar
1/2 tsp. sea salt
1 tsp. vanilla
2 tbsp. nutritional yeast (optional for cheesecake flavor)
2 cups strawberries

Instructions:

Add all liquids to the blender first and then add all other ingredients. Combine in a high-speed blender and blend until smooth and creamy.

Assembly:

Spray the pie pan with non-stick oil spray. Firmly shape the crust to the pie pan. Add the filling on top of the crust. Put the pie pan in the freezer and allow the crust to become firm (3-5 hours). Garnish with fresh strawberries, coconut flakes and almond slices or whatever your heart desires.

WHITE CHOCOLATE PIE

Equipment:

High-speed blender
Food processor S-Blade
Measuring cups and spoons
Bowls
Spatula
Pie pan

Products:

Cashews (1-2 bags)
Organic coconut milk or organic almond milk
Cocoa butter (1lb block)
Vanilla extract
Agave nectar
Sea Salt
Coconut oil
Hemp granola (1-2 bags depending on size)

Crust:

2 1/2 cups hemp granola
1 cup white chocolate parfait mix

Mix well until granola is coated. Place the granola on the bottom and the sides of a 1/4 inch thick

White Chocolate Pie Filling:

1 cup non-dairy almond or coconut milk
2 1/2 cups raw soaked and rinsed cashews
3/4 cups agave nectar
1/2 cup melted cocoa butter
1 tsp. vanilla extract
1/2 tsp. sea salt

Instructions:
Add all liquids to the blender first and then add all other ingredients. Combine in a high-speed blender and blend until smooth and creamy.

Assembly:
Spray the pie pan with non-stick oil spray. Firmly shape the crust to the pie pan, add the filling on top of the crust. Put the pie pan the freezer and allow the crust to become firm (3-5 hours). Garnish with extra crust if desired.

CHOCOLATE COCONUT CREAM PIE

Equipment:

- High-speed blender
- Food processor S-Blade
- Measuring cups and spoons
- Bowls
- Spatula
- Pie pan

Product:

- Cashews
- Organic coconut milk in the can
- Shredded coconut (1 bag)
- Ripe avocado (4)
- Agave nectar
- Sea salt
- Cocoa butter (approx 1lb)
- Cocoa powder
- Vanilla extract
- Hemp granola

Crust:

- 1 cup shredded coconut
- 2 1/2 cups hemp granola
- 1 cup dried and processed cashews

Place all ingredients in the food processor using the S-Blade and break the nuts down to a grainy consistency.

Chocolate Coconut Cream Pie Filling:

- 1 can organic coconut milk (cream plus milk)
- 4 ripe avocados
- 1/2 cup agave nectar (sweeten to taste)
- 1/2 cup cocoa powder

1/2 cup melted cocoa butter
1 tsp. vanilla extract
1 tsp. sea salt

Instructions:
Add all liquids to the blender first and then all other ingredients. Combine in a high-speed blender and blend until smooth and creamy.

Assembly:
Spray the pie pan with non-stick oil spray. Firmly shape the crust to the pie pan. Add filling on top of the crust. Put in the freezer and allow to become firm (3-5 hours).

Life is too short not to enjoy delicious treats - make sure to keep sweet things in our life.

--**Chef Babette**

CHAPTER 4
Ice Box Cakes

CHOCOLATE BUNDT CAKE

Equipment:

High-speed blender
Food processor
12 cup Bundt pan
Spatula

Products:

Raw walnuts
Raw cashews
Cocoa powder
Cocoa butter (approx 1lb)
Coconut oil
Agave nectar
Avocados (3-4)
Sea salt
Non-stick coconut oil spray

Chocolate Cake Base:

2 cups walnuts
3 cups cashews
1 cup cocoa powder
1/2 tsp. sea salt

Process all ingredients in a food processor using the S Blade. Process leaving the cake slightly grainy, then transfer to a mixing bowl. Set aside.

Cake Filling - Chocolate Pudding:

3-4 ripe avocados (the riper the better… dark spots are desired)
1/2 cup melted coconut oil
3/4 cup agave nectar
1/3 cup melted cocoa butter
1/4 cup cocoa powder
1 tsp. sea salt

Blend all ingredients until smooth and creamy.

Building the Cake:
Using a 12-cup Bundt pan, spray coconut oil in the pan. Layer with 2 cups of chocolate pudding. Add a layer of the nut cake mix and repeat layers until the Bundt pan is full (last layer should be pudding). Place the Bundt pan in freezer for 2-3 hours or until solid.

Removing Bundt:
I have found the easiest way to remove the Bundt cake is to turn the pan upside down on desired dish/plate and use a hot towel to cover the Bundt pan. When the Bundt cake becomes loose enough, then lift the pan.

Topping:
Remember, the dessert is a canvas. Make it your masterpiece! I like to top this one with the chocolate cocoa nibs for garnish.

***Note: This cake is awesome with fruit. I suggest stuffing the hole of the Bundt cake with your favorite. Suggestions for this Bundt cake; bananas, blackberries, blueberries, raspberries, peanut butter caramel sauce.

It's never to late to begin your journey to a better and healthier you -

--**Chef Babette**

BLUEBERRY BUNDT CAKE

Equipment:

- High-speed blender
- Food processor
- 12 cup Bundt pan
- Spatula

Product:

- Raw walnuts (1-2 bags depending on size)
- Raw cashews (1-2 bags depending on size)
- Granola
- Freeze dried blueberries (1 bag)
- Fresh blueberries (1 large bag)
- Non-dairy milk
- Coconut oil
- Agave nectar
- Lemons
- Sea salt
- Non-stick coconut oil spray

Blueberry Cake:

- 2 cups walnuts
- 2 cups granola
- 2 bags freeze dried blueberries

Process all ingredients in a food processor using the S Blade. Transfer to a mixing bowl and set aside.

Cake Filling - ***Blueberry Parfait***

- 1 cup non-dairy milk
- 3/4 cup agave nectar
- 2 tbsp. lemon juice
- 1/4 cup coconut oil
- 3 cups soaked and rinsed cashews

2 cups fresh blueberries
1 bag freeze dried blueberries
1/2 tsp. sea salt

Instructions:
Add all liquids to the blender first and then add all other ingredients. Combine in a high-speed blender and blend until smooth and creamy.

Building the Cake:
Using a 12 cup Bundt pan, spray the coconut oil in the pan with 2 cups of blueberry pudding. Add a layer of the nut cake mix and repeat layers until the Bundt pan is full (last layer should be pudding). Set the Bundt pan in the freezer for 2-3 hours or until solid.

Removing The Bundt:
I have found the easiest way to remove the Bundt cake is to turn the pan upside down on desired dish/plate and use a hot towel to cover the top of the Bundt pan. When the Bundt becomes loose enough, lift the pan.

Topping:
Garnish with desired fruit or cashew crumble (see page number?) and serve.

RAW CARROT CAKE

Equipment:

High-speed blender
Food processor
4 - 3" or 4" molds
Bowls
Spoons
Spatula

Product:

Raw walnuts (1-2 bags depending on size)
Raw cashews (1-2 bags depending on size)
Lemons
Non-dairy milk
Cocoa powder
Coconut oil
Agave nectar
Almond flour
Raisins (1lb)
Diced Pineapple (1)
Shredded carrots (1lb)
Nutmeg
Sea salt
Non-stick coconut oil spray

Cake Mix (dry nut mixture)

3 cups walnuts
2 tsp. nutmeg
2 tbsp. almond flour
1/2 cup raisins
1/2 cup shredded carrots
1/2 cup diced pineapple

Process the walnuts, almond flour, nutmeg and sea salt in a food processor using the S Blade. Break the ingredients down to a fine grainy consistency. Transfer to a bowl and add the carrots, raisins and pineapple. Mix well and set aside.

Filling:
See recipe for Lemon parfait mix (pg. 25).
2 cups pineapple

Blend all ingredients and blend until smooth and creamy.

Building the Cake:
Set 1 cup of cake mix aside to dress the top of the cake Place the 3" molds on a cookie sheet and lightly spray with non- stick coconut oil spray. Add 1/3 cup cake mix to each mold (press mix into mold evenly). Layer with diced pineapple. Pour 1/4 cup filling over pineapple (fill to 1/4 inch from the top). Place molds in freezer for 2-3 hours or until solid.

Removing the Molds:
I have found the easiest way to remove the cake from the mold use a hot towel to warm the sides of the molds. When the molds becomes loose enough, gently press top of dessert and let it slide out.

To Decorate:
To garnish, sprinkle the extra cake mix and shredded carrots on top of the cake.

Who said you can't have your cake and eat it too? Not me.

--Chef Babette

PEANUT POWER CAKE:

Equipment:

- High-speed blender
- Food processor
- 5 - 3" or 4" molds
- Bowls
- Spoons
- Spatula

Product:

- Cashews
- Non-dairy milk
- Coconut oil
- Agave nectar
- Sea salt
- Non-stick coconut oil spray
- Creamy peanut butter
- Vanilla extract
- Yams (1-2 yams depending on size)

Cake Crust:

- 2 cups raw/dry cashew pieces
- 1/4 cup peanut butter parfait mix (see below)

Process the cashews in a food processor using the S-Blade until the cashews are a grainy consistency. Transfer the mixture to a mixing bowl. Add 1/4 cup of parfait mix Mix well and set aside.

Peanut Butter Parfait Mix

- 1 cup non-dairy milk
- 3/4 cup agave nectar
- 1/4 cup coconut oil
- 1 cup creamy peanut butter
- 1/2 tsp. sea salt

1 tsp. vanilla extract
1 cup yams cooked or raw
3 1/2 cups raw soaked cashews

Instructions:
Add all liquids to the blender first and then add all other ingredients. Combine in a high-speed blender and blend until smooth and creamy.

Place five 3 or 4-inch molds on a cookie sheet. Spray each mold with non-stick coconut oil spray.

Building the Cake:
Add 1/4 cup cake mix to each mold
Add 1/3 cups parfait mix
Add extra cake mix to the top of the cake and a dollop of creamy peanut butter Freeze until solid.

Removing The Molds
I have found the easiest way to remove the molds is to use a hot towel and wrap around the mold until cake is loose then gently push cake onto plate.

***Note: This recipe is made using a 4 qt casserole pan. If using a larger casserole pan or Bundt pan, the recipe should be doubled.

Equipment:

High-speed blender
Food processor
4 quart casserole dish
Bowls
Spoons
Spatula

Products:

Granola (1 bag)
Cocoa powder
Avocados (3)
Cashews (1 bag depending on size)
Non-dairy milk
Coconut oil
Agave nectar
Freeze dried raspberries
Carob chips
Vanilla extract
Sea salt
Non-stick coconut oil spray

Cake Crust:

2 cups of your favorite granola (no raisins or other fruit/nuts)
2 cups - walnuts
1/2 tsp. sea salt
1/2 cup cocoa powder

Process ingredients in a food processor using the S-Blade. The crust should be broken down to a powdery consistency. Put in a bowl and add 1/4 to 1/2 cup of agave nectar, (depending on how sweet your taste buds are). Use a spoon and blend well.

Spray a casserole dish with non-stick coconut oil spray and press some (not all) of the crust mixture to fill the bottom layer of the casserole dish.

Filling:

1 cup non dairy milk
1 cup agave nectar
1/4 cup of coconut oil (preferably melted) if not melted soft
1 tsp,. sea salt
1/2 cup of cocoa powder
1 tsp. of vanilla extract
3 avocados (ripe or over ripe they can have black spots)
1 cup of soaked avocados
2 packs freeze dried raspberries
1 package carob chips

Instructions:

Add all liquids to the blender first and then add all other ingredients. Combine in a high-speed blender and blend until smooth and creamy.

Building the Cake:

Spray the casserole dish with non-stick oil spray.

***Note: Do not use all of the filling or crust for 1st layer, as you will need to repeat them.

Layer 1 - Spread crust evenly in the bottom of the casserole dish.
Layer 2 - Using an offset spatula, (or the back of a spoon) spread a thin layer of chocolate onto the crust.
Layer 3 - Crumble two bags of freeze dried raspberries with your fingers over the filling
Layer 4 - Sprinkle a layer of carob chips on top.

Place the cake in the freezer and allow to firm for 30 minutes.. Place the remaining chocolate filling and crust mixture in the refrigerator for 30 minutes as well.

Repeat layers:
Layer 5 - Chocolate filling (this time layer should be thicker).
Layer 6 - Sprinkle additional crust on top
Layer 7 - Sprinkle additional carob chips on top.

Freeze until firm (2-3 hours). Drizzle berry compote (pg.138) on top if desired.

RASPBERRY / LEMON BUNDT CAKE

Equipment:

High-speed blender
Food processor
12 cup Bundt pan
Bowls
Spoons
Spatula

Products:

Granola (1-2 bags depending on size)
Lemons
Non-dairy milk
Coconut oil
Agave nectar
4 packs freeze dried raspberries
Blackberries
Vanilla extract
Sea salt
Non-stick coconut oil spray
Walnuts
Cashews

Filling:

Lemon parfait (pg. 25)
Raspberry parfait (pg. 29)

After making the parfaits, put them in a container and refrigerate while making the other components to the recipe.

Berry Compote: See recipe pg. 138

Cake Crust:

3 cups walnuts

2 packs freeze dried raspberries
1 cup berry compote
2 cups granola

Place dried ingredients in a food processor using the S Blade. Process until slightly grainy. Transfer to a mixing bowl. Add 1 cup of berry compote. Mix well leaving the cake crust moist.

Building the Cake:
Spray the Bundt pan using non-oil spray. Using the food processor, process one package freeze dried raspberries. The result should be a grainy consistency.

Layer 1 - Add 1/2 the amount of freeze dried raspberries to bottom of Bundt pan
Layer 2 - Add cake crust
Layer 3 - Pour 3 cups lemon parfait filling on top of crust
Freeze (1-2 hours or until firm)
Layer 4 - Add 3 cups raspberry parfait mix

Place the cake back in the freezer until firm. I have found the easiest way to remove the Bundt cake is to turn the pan upside down on desired dish/plate and use a hot towel to cover the Bundt pan. When the Bundt cake becomes loose enough, then lift the pan. Use the remainder of the compote to decorate your cake.

CHAPTER 5

Ice Box Cobblers

BERRY BLUE COBBLER

Equipment:

3” or 4” mold
High-speed blender
Measuring spoons and cups
Food processor (S-Blade)
Citrus juicer
Spatula
Bowls

Products:

Cashews
Almonds
Pecans
Blueberries (raw and freeze dried)
Lemon
Agave nectar
Almond extract
Sea salt
Coconut oil
Baby Thai coconut (if coconuts are not available, you can substitute with organic coconut milk in the can).

Filling:

2 cups blueberries
1/4 cup freeze dried blueberries
1/4 cup agave nectar
1/2 tsp. almond extract
1/2 cup lemon juice
2 tbsp. blueberry parfait mix (from below)

Put all ingredients in a bowl and fold together. Set aside

Blueberry Parfait Mix Recipe:

1 cup lemon juice
1 Baby Thai coconut (water and flesh) or 1 can organic coconut milk
2 cups soaked and rinsed cashews
1/2 cup agave nectar
1/2 tsp. sea salt
1 tsp. lemon extract (optional)
1/4 cup coconut oil
2 cups fresh or frozen blueberries

Add all liquids to the blender first and then add all other ingredients. Combine in a high-speed blender and blend until smooth and creamy.

Crust:

1/2 cup cashews
1/4 cup almonds
1/4 cup pecans
1 cup freeze dried blueberries
2 tbsps. lemon juice
1 tsp. almond extract
2 tbsp. agave nectar

Using a food processor and an S-Blade, pulse all ingredients together. Empty the contents in a bowl and add 2 tbsp. of blueberry parfait mix to the crust mixture for moisture and flavor. Set aside.

Assembly:

Spray mold with non stick oil spray. The idea is to layer the dessert in your mold and remember you are creating an edible masterpiece!

Layer 1- Crust mixture (1/4 inch)
Layer 2- Add blueberry filling (1/4 inch)
Layer 3- Top crust mixture (1/4 inch)
Layer 4- Decorate with your favorite fruit or freeze extra parfait mix and scoop on top like ice cream. (See photo)

Removing The Molds

I have found the easiest way to remove the molds is to use a hot towel and wrap around the mold until the cake is loose, then gently push the cake onto the plate.

Instead of cutting out what you love to eat because tt no longer loves you back? Flip that dish and make what you love crave your attention.

--Chef Babette

INEZ, FRANCIS, LULA, CARRIE, MARGARET, LEE CREAMY PEACH COBBLER

Ok, I know you're asking yourself, "what the hell kind of a name is that?" Well, that was my southern momma's full name and this peach cobbler is an ode to my sweet momma. You will enjoy a light creamy cobbler with fresh peaches and I pray that every bite fills your spirit with joy!

Equipment:

3" or 4" mold
High-speed blender
Measuring spoons and cups
Food processor (S-Blade)
Citrus juicer
Spatula
Bowls

Products:

1 Baby Thai coconut
Cashews
Rolled oats (1 or 2 bags depending on size)
Agave nectar
3 cups peaches (fresh or frozen)
Coconut oil
Almond extract
Vanilla powder
Sea salt
Lemons

Peach Cobbler Filling:

2 cups fresh peaches
1 Baby Thai coconut
2 cups soaked cashews
2 tbsp. coconut oil
1/2 tsp. sea salt
1 tsp. almond extract

1 tsp. vanilla powder

Add all liquids to the blender first and then add all other ingredients. Combine in a high-speed blender and blend until smooth and creamy. Dice 1 cup of peaches and add to the filling. Set aside.

Crust:

3 cups rolled oats
1 cup dry cashews
2 tbsp. lemon juice
1 tsp. almond extract
1/4 cup peach cobbler filling
2 tbsp. agave nectar
1 pinch sea salt

Put rolled oats in a bowl, set aside. Grind the dry cashews in food processor using the S-blade until they have reached a slightly granulated consistency—DO NOT GRIND THEM INTO POWDER. Add them to the oats along with the rest of the dry

Ingredients.

Add the wet ingredients along with a 1/4 cup of filling and fold all the ingredients together and set aside.

Assembly:

Spray mold with non stick oil spray and layer as follows:

Layer 1- Crust mixture (1/4 inch)
Layer 2- Add filling (1/4 inch)
Layer 3- Top crust mixture (1/4 inch)
Layer 4- Decorate with your favorite fruit or freeze extra parfait mix and scoop on top like ice cream.

Removing The Molds

I have found the easiest way to remove the molds is to use a hot towel and wrap around the mold until cake is loose then gently push cake onto plate.

*Note: Have fun with this dessert. If you desire more texture, go for it! Add slivered almonds or extra fruit.

Transforming the unhealthy into the healthy makes for a guilt-free, delicious swallow.

---Chef Babette

ROCKIN' RASPBERRY COBBLER:

Raspberries ROCK!!! I never really admired raspberries until I experimented with this cobbler. This particular cobbler bursts with flavors, especially when it is mixed with rolled oats. There is a fusion of creamy, sweet, tartness that tantalizes your taste buds. I am currently working on my foodie verbiage for my readers, because I usually just say, "this shit rocks!"

Equipment:

Food processor
High-speed blender
Measuring cups
Wooden spoons
Fork
Whisk
Bowls
Scraper
3" or 4" mold

Products:

Rolled Oats (1-2 bags depending on size)
Cashews
Lemons
Fresh Raspberries (1 bag)
Freeze dried raspberries (1 bag)
Agave nectar
Raw coconut oil

Layer 1-(Bottom Crust)

2 cups rolled oats
2 tbsp. lemon juice
¼ cup agave nectar
1 cup fresh raspberries
1 cup ground cashews
½ cup freeze dried raspberries

Pour rolled oats into a bowl, Add additional ingredients and fold with a spoon or your hands until the oats are moistened evenly. This should create a cookie dough type consistency. Set aside.

Layer 2-(Filling)

Please see raspberry parfait recipe pg. 29

Layer 3- (Top Crust)

1 cup ground cashews
Freeze dried raspberries (great to kick up the flavor but if you can't find them use fresh or frozen).
1 tbsp. coconut oil
1 tbsp. agave nectar
1 tbsp. lemon juice

Grind cashews in food processor using the S-blade. In a bowl, add all ingredients and fold with a spoon. Spray mold with non stick oil spray. The idea is to layer the dessert in your mold and remember you are creating an edible masterpiece!

Assembly:

Layer 1- Bottom Crust - 1/4 " the width of the mold
Layer 2- Filling - Fill mold with filling and leave a 1/4" room at top of mold
Layer 3- Top Crust - Just enough to cover the filling

Removing The Molds

I have found the easiest way to remove the molds is to use a hot towel and wrap around the mold until cake is loose then gently push cake onto plate.

Garnish with fresh berries. Enjoy!

Eat life to sustain life.
-- Chef Babette

CREAMY, CRUMBLE, APPLE COBBLER:

I used to love apple pie when I was little as well as apple turnovers, apple pie, and apple cobbler. I don't believe that I've ever disliked anything containing apples. I remember warming up any one of those desserts that would be complimented with a nice big scoop of vanilla ice cream. The idea for this dessert is to be able to combine the, "yummy goodness" of the cobbler with a creamy filling that will replace the ice cream. No guilt here, only pleasure.

Equipment:

8" inch pie dish
High-speed blender
Measuring spoons and cups
Food processor (S-Blade)
Citrus juicer
Spatula

Products:

Cashews (1 bag)
Pistachios (1 bag)
Almonds (1 bag)
Apples (your favorite- 2-3 depending on size)
Dried apples (1 bag)
Lemon
Agave nectar
Raw coconut oil (optional)
Vanilla powder
Sea salt
Almond extract
Almond butter
Pitted dates

Apple Cobbler Filling:

1 cup apple parfait mix (see Apple Parfait recipe pg. 34)
Add 2 cups diced and peeled apples, set aside.
Blend until smooth and creamy.

Middle Creamy Mixture:

1 tbsp. almond butter
1/2 cup soaked and pitted dates
1/2 tsp. sea salt

In the food processor pulse almond butter, dates and sea salt until smooth and creamy. Set aside.

Crust:

1 cup pistachios
1/4 cup almonds
1/4 cup cashews
1/2 cup dates
1 tsp. almond extract
1 tsp. vanilla powder

In a food processor using the S-Blade, pulse ingredients until you achieve a granular consistency. Set aside.

Topping:

1/2 cup pistachios
1/2 cup cashews
1/2 cup dates
1/2 tsp. vanilla powder
1 pinch of sea salt

Combine all ingredients in the food processor and pulse until you achieve a sticky, crumbly consistency.

Assembly:

Spray the pie pan with non-oil spray. Press the crust in the bottom of the pie pan. (For more crust add more nuts and dates). Spread the middle creamy mixture on bottom of crust. Decorate the pie pan with thinly sliced apples in a fan style format. Add the filling and refrigerate for 20 minutes or until the filling stiffens. Top with topping.

CHAPTER 6
Ice Box Cookies

WHITE CHOCOLATE OATMEAL COOKIES

Equipment:

Cookie sheet
Mixing bowl
Measuring spoons

Products:

Organic rolled oats
Raw cashews
Non-dairy milk
Vanilla extract
Agave nectar
Coconut oil
Cocoa butter
Vegan cocoa chips
Sea salt
Non- stick coconut oil spray

Recipe:

2 cups rolled oats
1 cup chopped pecans
1/2 cup white chocolate parfait mix (pg. 37)
1/4 cup melted cocoa butter (see Tips and Tricks pg. 17)
1/2 tsp sea salt
1 cup vegan cocoa chips

Spray cookie sheet with non-stick oil spray. Mix all ingredients in a mixing bowl until sticky. Form into 1/4 cup balls and flatten into cookies. Place on cookie sheet and freeze.

DARK CHOCOLATE COOKIES

Equipment:

- Cookie sheet
- Mixing bowl
- Measuring spoons

Products:

- Raw walnuts
- Raw cashews
- Organic rolled oats
- Cocoa powder
- Agave nectar
- Coconut oil
- Sea salt

Recipe:

- 2 cups walnuts
- 1 cup cashews
- 2 cups rolled oats
- 1/2 cup cocoa powder
- 1/2 cup agave nectar
- 1 tbsp. coconut oil

Begin this recipe by processing the walnuts, cashews, cocoa powder and sea salt in a food processor using the S-Blade. Transfer to a mixing bowl and add agave nectar and coconut oil. Spray the cookie sheet with non-stick oil spray. Mix all ingredients until sticky. Form into 1/4 cup balls and flatten into cookies. Place the balls on the cookie sheet and freeze.

CHOCOLATE PECAN CASHEW COOKIES

Equipment:

Cookie sheet
Mixing bowl
Measuring spoons

Products:

Raw pecans
Raw cashews
Agave nectar
Cocoa butter
Carob chips
Sea salt
Non-stick spray oil

Recipe:

1 1/2 cups raw pecans
1/2 Raw cashews
1/2 tsp. sea salt
3 tbsp Agave nectar
1 tbsp melted cocoa butter
1 cup carob chips

Instructions:

Begin this recipe by processing the pecans, cashews, cocoa powder and sea salt in a food processor using the S-Blade. Transfer to a mixing bowl and add agave nectar, melted cocoa butter (see Tips, Tricks and Important Information section for tips on melting cocoa butter pg. 18), and carob chips, mix well. Form into 1/4 cup balls and flatten into cookies. Spray cookie sheet with non-stick oil, place on cookie sheet and freeze.

PEANUT BUTTER CASHEW COOKIES

*Note: This recipe requires dehydration for 16 hours

Equipment:

Cookie sheet
Mixing bowl
Measuring spoons
Dehydrator

Products:

Raw cashews
Raw peanuts
Organic (no salt) peanut butter
Almond flour
Agave nectar
Cinnamon
Sea salt
Non-stick oil

Recipe:

1/2 cup almond flour
1/2 raw cashews
1/2 cup raw peanuts
1/4 cup peanut butter
1 tsp. vanilla
1/2 tsp. sea salt
1 tsp. cinnamon
1/4 cup agave nectar

Instructions:

Begin this recipe by processing the peanuts, cashews, almond flour, cinnamon and sea salt in a food processor using the S-Blade. Transfer to a mixing bowl and add peanut butter, agave nectar and vanilla. Mix well and set aside a couple of hours to thicken. Form into 1/4 cup balls and flatten into cookies. Place cookies on a Teflex sheet and dehydrate.

OATMEAL CASHEWS RAISIN COOKIES

Equipment:

Cookie sheet
Mixing bowl
Measuring spoons

Products:

Organic rolled oats
Raw cashews
Raisins
Coconut oil
Agave nectar
Cinnamon
Non stick coconut oil spray
Organic apple juice or 2 large apples freshly squeezed

Recipe

2 cups gluten free organic rolled oats
1/2 cup finely chopped cashews
1/2 cup raisins
2 tbsp. coconut oil
1/2 cup agave nectar
1 tsp. cinnamon
1/2 cup apple juice

Instructions:

Spray the cookie sheet with non-stick oil spray. Mix all ingredients in a mixing bowl until sticky. Form into 1/4 cup balls and flatten into cookies. Place the balls on the cookie sheet and freeze.

CHAPTER 7
Neopolitian Ice Cream

Equipment for all 3 recipes:

High-speed blender
Spatula
Cup or bowl
Measuring cup
Measuring spoons
Juicer (for strawberry bold color- if you don't have a juicer see the Tips, Tricks and Important Information section pg 18).

Vanilla :

Ingredients:

1 cup coconut milk
1 cup agave
1/2 cups coconut oil
3 1/2 cups soaked cashews
1/2 tsp. sea salt
1 tbsp. vanilla extract

Instructions:

Add all liquids to the blender first and then add all other ingredients. Combine in a high-speed blender and blend until smooth and creamy, then freeze.

Strawberry:

1 cup coconut milk
1 cup agave
1/2 cups coconut oil
3 1/2 cups soaked cashews
15 organic strawberries (fresh or frozen)
1 tbsp. vanilla
1/2 tsp. sea salt
1/2 cup beet juice (if you don't have a juicer see the Tips, Tricks and Important Information section pg 18).

Instructions:

Add all liquids to the blender first and then add all other ingredients. Combine in a high-speed blender and blend until smooth and creamy, then freeze.

Chocolate:

- 1 cup coconut milk
- 1 cup agave
- 1/2 cup coconut oil
- 3 cups soaked and rinsed cashews
- 1/2 cup cacao powder
- 1 tbsp. vanilla
- 1/2 tsp. sea salt

Instructions:

Add all liquids to the blender first and then add all other ingredients. Combine in a high-speed blender and blend until smooth and creamy, then freeze.

Neapolitan: A combination of the above flavors

Instructions:

To make it Neapolitan, simply layer flavors. Add the 1st flavor and chill until solid, add the second flavor and chill until solid and add the final flavor, then freeze.

We all should bite into something new and decadent every now and then, What have you today my friend?
-- **Chef Babette**

CHAPTER 8
Accompaniments

CHOCOLATE GANACHE:

1/4 cup coconut oil
1/2 cup agave nectar
2-3 tbsp. cocoa powder
1 pinch sea salt

Blend ingredients together to make the Ganache

BERRY COMPOTE RECIPE:

1 cup raspberries
1 cup blackberries
1 package freeze dried raspberries
1/2 cup agave nectar

Blend together leaving the mixture slightly chunky.

CARAMEL SAUCE RECIPE:

1/2 cup agave nectar
2 cups soaked (pitted) dates
1 soft medium yam (boil)
1 tsp. sea salt
1 tbsp. vanilla extract
1/2 cup soft coconut oil

Add all ingredients to a blender and blend until creamy. To thin the caramel, add non-dairy milk and blend. Remember less is more.

BLUEBERRY COMPOTE RECIPE:

1/4 cup lemon juice
2 cups blueberries
1 package freeze dried blueberries
1/2 cup agave nectar
Add all ingredients to a blender and blend until creamy.

CHOCOLATE SYRUP:

Ingredients:

2 ripe avocados
3/4 cup agave nectar
1/4 cup cocao powder
1/4 cup melted coconut oil
a pinch sea salt

Add all ingredients to a blender and blend until "very" creamy.

CASHEWS CRUMBLE:

1 cup chopped cashews
1/4 cup caramel sauce (yams are not necessary- see recipe in this chapter)
2 tbsp. unsulfured shredded coconut
1 tsp. cinnamon
a pinch of sea salt

Instructions:

Combine all ingredients in a mixing bowl and stir until the nuts are completely coated. Spray a cookie sheet with non-stick oil spray and spread the crumble out evenly. Bake at 350 degrees for 20-25 minutes. Watch carefully. The idea is not to roast them but make them hard enough to crumble. Remove from the oven and allow to chill. Transfer to a mixing bowl and use the bottom of a glass jar to crumble the cashew pieces. Store in a glass jar and use as a topping.

Chef Babette's Reading Recommensations:

Literary Recommendations:
Fit for Life by Harvey and Marilyn Diamond - Fit for Life was instrumental in my transformation. It is the first book I've listed, and for good reason. It's an easy read, it is very informative and it appeals to your common sense. When I began my journey from meat eater to vegan, I kept this book by my side as though it was my vegan Bible. It's a great book to start the learning process and to gain an understanding the importance of conscious eating.

The Mucusless Diet by Professor Arnold Eheret - The information in this book is priceless. Most of us don't realize the danger that mucus can cause in our bodies. Dr. Eheret provides a wealth of information about mucus forming foods and their detrimental effect on our bodies.
The Raw Food Detox Diet by Natalia Rose - This book hits the nail on the head when it comes to great recipes and following a detox system that aids in weight loss. I've sampled several of the recipes which have all turned out great. The book is easy to follow and offers a great alternative to fasting.

Living Raw Food by Sarma Melngailis - This is one of my all-time favorite books!
Rawvolution by Matt Amsden - Matt is brilliant when it comes to RAW food. His spirit is definitely in the right place. The book is visually appealing and the recipes are especially pleasing to the palate.

Superfoods by David Wolfe - This is a great find. It dives into a plethora of unbelievable nutrient rich foods that are designed to heal the body.

ENZYMES… The Fountain of Life by D.A. Lopez, M.D., et. al…-BLURB

Professional References
Dr. Gary Null - Progressive Radio Network-http://www.garynull.com/
Dr. Lodi - (Oasis of Healing)-http://www.anoasisofhealing.com/
Dr. Rabb - http://www.drnathanrabb.com/
Dr. Baxter Montgomery
Dr. Farid Zarif

Online References:

Raw Pantry Essentials
http://thehappyrawkitchen.blogspot.com/2010/08/raw-pantry-essentials.html

Cashews
http://www.whfoods.com/genpage.php?pfriendly=1&tname=foodspice&dbid=98

31895284R00082

Made in the USA
San Bernardino, CA
08 April 2019